A DISSIMULATION
OF BIRDS

Illustrated Collective Nouns of Birds

Steve Palin

MINERVA PRESS
LONDON
ATLANTA MONTREUX SYDNEY

A DISSIMULATION OF BIRDS
Copyright © Steve Palin 1998

ISBN 0 75410 290 4

First Published 1998 by
MINERVA PRESS
195 Knightsbridge
London SW7 1RE

Printed in Great Britain for Minerva Press

A DISSIMULATION
OF BIRDS

Illustrated Collective Nouns of Birds

Introduction

There are many nouns in the English language which describe groups or collections. These are commonly called collective nouns: a *band* of musicians, a *pack* of cards, a *troupe* of dancers, etc. These nouns are also known as group or company terms, or nouns of assembly. Some of the most interesting apply to living creatures – especially animals and birds. These particular nouns are referred to as *terms of venery* (venery being the sport or practice of hunting). Many of these have their origins in the hunting or sporting language of the Middle Ages and may be regarded as genuine. Some may be the result of errors in printing or copying of the originals. There are undoubtedly some which have their origins in the inventions and affectations of the fanciful.

Most people are familiar with the term *a flock of birds*, some with *a skein of geese* or even *a covey of partridge*, but how many of us would know the company term for a group of woodpeckers or woodcock?

A number of books from the time of the Middle Ages began recording such terms; indeed it was a requirement of certain social classes that the correct terminology was employed. One could be embarrassed amongst one's peers if an incorrect collective was used!

Perhaps the most significant of these books was *The Book of St Albans*, written by Dame Juliana Barnes, the prioress of a certain convent. As this book was written in 1486, it is difficult to verify the claim by some that there was no such prioress and Dame Juliana Barnes was an invention. Whatever the truth about the author, the book, containing three *treatises* on hawking, hunting and heraldry, certainly became an authoritative reference source.

The Book of St Albans was not considered to be completely original, however. It relied for much of its information upon another work: *Le Art de Venerie* (sic) by William Twici, published circa 1328. Twici was Edward II's huntsman and this is the oldest known hunting book in England. It was reprinted in 1843 and in the intervening period there were many other books on the subject.

There is little doubt that in those early days scribes and printers were guilty of some miscopying. Together with the natural evolution of language, this gave rise to variations of terms which, although phonetically similar, may be semantically quite different; for example, the group term for herons and bitterns is recorded as a *siege* or a *sedge*.

More recent works on the subject include C.E. Hare's book *The Language of Sport* (1939) and James Lipton's *An Exaltation of Larks or The Venereal Game* (1970). Both are excellent and any reader wanting a more academic insight into the history and status of terms could do no better than read these two books. Lists of collective nouns, however, appear in many different volumes: schoolchildren's grammar books, crossword companions, anthologies and so on. In my experience no two such lists are alike; words which are contained in one may be missed out from another. The list which appears at the back of *this* book is a compilation of every group term for birds known to me, even though the status and origins of each may be different.

The purpose of this book, though, is *not* an academic one. People better qualified than I have already provided the academic and historical perspective on nouns of assembly. But these words are *fun*! Indeed, the second part of Lipton's book title relates to a game in which anyone can *invent* collective nouns! Whatever the origin or lexicographic status of a term, it always arouses interest. This book seeks simply to provide a comprehensive list of collective nouns for birds, and to illustrate some of them.

The verb to *dissimulate* means to pretend, or to conceal one's real feelings. The collective noun *dissimulation*, first referred to in the Egerton manuscript of about 1452, is applied particularly to flocks of *small* birds. It is said to derive from the habit many such birds have of distracting predators from the nest by their diverting behaviour or pretended injury.

Bevy
of quail

The collective noun for quails is long established. It was first recorded in the Egerton manuscript of the mid-fifteenth century and then in *The Book of St Albans* of 1486. *Bevy* is a true company term and has also been applied to larks, although C.E. Hare in *The Language of Sport* considers this may have been an error on the part of an early scribe. (*Bevy* is also recorded as a company term for roe deer and 'ladies'!)

The quail is not only our smallest game bird, but also the only one which migrates. It spends the months from May to September breeding and raising its young here, before wintering in Africa. Many are shot and trapped during their journey over the Mediterranean and North African countries, and this is no doubt a factor in the quail's falling numbers. Although the British population can fluctuate from year to year, quail remain scarce and confine themselves mainly to the southern counties.

Quail are the antithesis to the stereotype of the model child, being more often heard than seen. They are shy, secretive birds, difficult to flush and seldom seen on the ground. They do, however, have a characteristic three-syllabled call, sometimes translated as 'wet-my-lips', which is persistently repeated at dawn and dusk. 'Wet-my-lips' is a local name for the quail in Norfolk.

Even in an area where quail are known to be, an opportunity to make use of the collective noun is rare; it is only on migration that the birds form small flocks. At other times they are usually solitary.

Cast of hawks

The term *cast* is pure sporting terminology; it is used in relation only to birds *cast* from the fist in falconry or hawking. Moreover, the term relates only to a *pair* of birds being cast. If there were three, the group would be referred to as a *leash*.

The word *leash* is also the specific collective noun for the 'ladies' falcon', or merlin. Goshawks too have their own specific term. The goshawk was the yeoman's bird, and was 'let fly' rather than cast. Its collective noun is consequently a *flight* of goshawks.

An alternative term for *cast* is *couple*. This term may also be used for other birds of prey. *Cast*, *flight* and *leash* (meaning three) appeared in *The Book of St Albans* in 1486. The use of *leash* as a term for merlin first appeared in another fifteenth-century manuscript written by Harley.

The birds illustrated are sparrowhawks; the larger brown female is in flight on the left and the smaller grey/blue male on the right. At one time only certain species of birds could be flown by particular social classes or groups, hence the title of the 1960s novel *A Kestrel for a Knave*.

Except for *convocation*, a collective noun which is applied to eagles (of a somewhat questionable source), there seems to be no other collective noun for birds of prey apart from those above, which are falconry-related. This is despite the fact that many raptors are gregarious, often forming quite large groups.

Charm of finches

The term *charm* is a particularly interesting one. Appearing first in the Egerton manuscript of the mid-fifteenth century as *chyrme*, and subsequently in *The Book of St Albans* as *cherme*, it is a variant of the Old English world *cirm*. It has many modern variations: the current dictionary definition of *chirm*, for example, is to chirp or chirrup like birds. Another definition is a group of goldfinches: certainly the term *charm* is commonly believed to refer to the *noise* produced by finches.

Whilst many collective nouns have fallen into almost total disuse, reference is still occasionally made to a *charm* of finches. Whilst one school of thought applies it exclusively to the illustrated goldfinch, another allows for its use for finches in general. (A *trimming* and a *trembling* are other collective nouns for goldfinches.)

Certainly it is appropriate to have a collective noun for finches. Finches generally, as well as goldfinches specifically, are highly gregarious. They often group together in large flocks, particularly outside the breeding season. The greater the food source, the larger the flock. They are often very vocal when in such groups, thus explaining the collective noun. Although many finches will form flocks of mixed finch species, the goldfinch usually associates only with others of its kind.

Finches are primarily seed-eating birds and the goldfinch is no exception, preferring the seeds of herbs and flowering plants to those of grasses. The goldfinch also prefers to eat half-ripe or *milky* seed to dried seed. It is common across most of the British Isles, but scarcer in the far north.

Chime
of wrens

Small in stature but big in heart, the wren must rank as one of Britain's favourite and most abundant birds. Its song in spring pours forth with such vigour that it can drown out those of much larger species. Our national bird, appearing on the old farthing coin, the wren is steeped in ritual and folklore. Not all of it is supportive of the wren; the once-traditional Yuletide Wren Hunt, for example, would seem to contradict its proclaimed place in our hearts.

Chime is only one of two collective nouns applied to the wren. The term *herd* is almost certainly the older (appearing in *The Book of St Albans* in 1486) and indeed the more common reference. One explanation for this latter term is that the wren was afforded the same noun of assembly as that used for the hart or royal stag, being considered a 'royal' bird itself: in the Greek story of the wren and the eagle, the wren cunningly outwits the eagle in a flying competition to earn the royal title of King of Birds. *Herd* is also the collective noun for curlew (see Herd of Curlew).

The term *chime*, relayed to the author but not referred to in any authoritative text, is perhaps a reference to the similarity between the bell-ringer's tones and the cascading notes or cadences of the wren.

The wren is at times gregarious: large numbers of wrens have been recorded together on migrational flights (migration activity takes place mainly at the northern extent of its range). The most interesting aspect of wrens grouping together, however, is during periods of cold weather, when numbers may huddle and roost together for warmth.

Descent of woodpeckers

There are three species of resident British woodpecker: the great spotted, lesser spotted and the green. Of the three, the largest and most colourful is the illustrated green woodpecker. It is likely that the habits of this *particular* woodpecker gave rise to the company term, as it *descends* to the ground more frequently than the other two species. It does so to feed on its favourite food of ants, although sometimes it also feeds in trees. (Green woodpeckers have also been recorded *anting*, whereby the bird places ants amongst its feathers for the purpose of cleaning the plumage.)

The term *descent* may also arise from the ability of the green woodpecker to *descend* a tree, moving backwards down the trunk with its head uppermost. The third possible derivative of the term is the bird's occasional habit of moving from tree to tree, swooping downwards from the top of one to the base of another in the manner of a treecreeper.

Descent therefore is one of a number of collective nouns which relate to the habits or characteristics of a particular bird. The term was first recorded as *discecion* in a book called *The Hors, Shepe, & the Ghoos* printed in 1476 by Caxton.

One is unlikely to see a company of woodpeckers, however, as they are usually solitary birds. The exception to this general rule is perhaps during the breeding season when family groups may be seen in or around the nest site.

This evocative collective noun, dating from the fifteenth century, was used by James Lipton for the title of his 1968 book, *An Exaltation of Larks or The Venereal Game*. C.E. Hare, however, in his authoritative work, *The Language of Sport*, points out that the term is a fanciful, if long-standing name for larks in flight. Rather than being a true company term, it refers only to larks which soar into the sky and sing. The correct term for a number of larks is *flight*, a term derived from the lark's characteristic behaviour when disturbed. Larks often socialise in large numbers.

There are many types of lark throughout the world. Only two have regularly nested in Britain: the skylark and the now rare woodlark. The illustrated shore lark (sometimes known in Lancashire as a *snowflake*) is a regular winter visitor to British coastlines but has only bred here sporadically. The ringed plover was once popularly termed the 'sand lark'. The corn bunting likewise was known as the 'scribbling lark', so named because of the pattern of 'scribbled' lines on its eggs. Neither of these birds, of course, is a true lark.

The larks most likely to be seen taking to the air to sing are skylarks. Our commonest lark, they are today experiencing a serious decline in numbers. Primarily responsible are the changing farming practices which affect the habitat in which they breed. At one time they were so common that they were killed in large numbers to eat, as well as being caged as songbirds. (They would often be blinded in the mistaken belief that their song would thus be improved.) It would indeed be a tragedy if the exultant song of this bird, once a ubiquitous feature of any spring walk in the countryside and the inspiration for countless poems, was lost to future generations.

Fall
of woodcock

Woodcock are technically wading birds adapted to nesting and spending much of their time on the woodland and forest floor. The woodcock has long been a favourite sporting quarry, usually flushed by dog or beater as its camouflage inclines it to sit tight unless in immediate danger.

The term *fall* could refer both to its end of flight 'collapse' as it quickly drops to the ground and lands, or its reported habit of being sighted in numbers in the morning at places empty of woodcock the previous evening. (Woodcock are *crepuscular*, or active by dawn and dusk, so this phenomenon is quite feasible.) In this respect, reports that there had been a *fall of woodcock* would be in the same sense that there might have been a *fall of snow*.

Woodcock would not ordinarily be seen in groups, being typically solitary birds. There are times when more than one might be seen, however; for example, during a shoot where ground is being beaten, numbers of birds can often be seen in the air together. Whilst some woodcock are with us all year round, a degree of migratory movement does take place. Although they usually travel singly, they may occasionally be seen in pairs and very rarely in groups. In a good-sized wood, one can sometimes see and hear more than one woodcock performing their display flight, known as roding. They are, however, performing individually and not in a group.

Woodcock are so well camouflaged that it is sometimes difficult to see *one*, let alone many; for the birdwatcher, therefore, the collective noun for woodcock may only infrequently be required!

Gaggle of geese

The collective nouns for geese are similar to those for ducks in that both ducks and geese are collectively termed wildfowl. Thus the company terms *trip*, *sord*, *sute* and *plump* are common to both ducks and geese. *Gaggle* is a term specific to geese. Some authorities hold that it relates to geese only on land; others that it is those geese that are on land *or* water but not in the air. A number of geese in the air may be referred to as a *skein*, a *team* or a *wedge*. Mention has also been made of a *lag* of geese.

The term *gaggle* was first referred to as *gagelynge* in the Egerton manuscript of 1452. It has been claimed that it was one of those artificial and fanciful inventions of the fifteenth century, although it does refer to the noise made by geese. Its contemporary dictionary definition includes reference to a *knot* (see *knot* of waterfowl) of garrulous people, which can be likened to a flock of cackling geese. Whether fanciful or genuine, *gaggle* has stayed with us as a recognised term for geese when many other collectives have been lost through time.

The geese in the illustration are barnacle geese. These birds have a fascinating folklore. People at one time believed that they did indeed grow from barnacles. Medieval literature contains accounts of people claiming to be eyewitnesses to the hatching of the young geese from barnacle shells!

Barnacle geese are small grazing geese which breed in the Arctic and overwinter in Britain, mainly in Scotland and Ireland.

Herd of curlew

The haunting, liquid call of the curlew is synonymous with the winter foreshore and marsh. It is as well known to the farmer, however, as it is to the wildfowler, and anyone who has seen groups of this bird, the largest British wader, on meadows or fields will readily understand the collective noun *herd*.

The term can be traced as far back as any collective noun, appearing in *The Book of St Albans* in the fifteenth century. At that time, curlews were regularly eaten (along with many other birds which we would not think of eating today!). The idea of curlews providing a source of meat lends even more credence to the term *herd*.

Although not unique, the long slender bill of the curlew, used for probing into soft ground for its invertebrate food, is distinctive. The mottled brown plumage, its protection as a ground-nesting bird, is darker in the summer than in the winter. The curlew's name represents the sound of its call.

Solitary curlews are commonly seen, but they are also often gregarious. Flocks can sometimes consist of several thousand birds at non-breeding times, but even during the breeding season, groups of mature birds will sometimes associate with each other for feeding and roosting.

Knob
of waterfowl

Other birds could replace the moorhens in this illustration, as the term *knob* can refer to many species. Indeed it may refer to groups of varied wildfowl or waterfowl (wildfowl usually meaning ducks, geese or swans; waterfowl usually being a wider, more vague term for freshwater aquatic birds), or particular individual species. Different books and authors identify a *knob* of pochard, widgeon or teal. In addition, some authorities stipulate that a *knob* must be less than thirty birds. A *little knob* has been described as being between ten and twenty birds. If there are more than thirty wildfowl, some say, the terms *bunch*, *trip*, *plump*, *sord* or *sute* should be used, but this is by no means a universal opinion. Furthermore, *rush* is an alternative collective noun for pochard, *company* for widgeon and *spring* an alternative for teal. Just one reference has been made to a *coil* of teal and in the air, widgeon and others are referred to as a *flight*. Make sure you get the correct word the next time you're feeding the ducks!

It would seem that the term *knob* is a relatively recent one. It appeared in *The Complete Crossword Reference Book* by C. Thorn in 1932, and in *Nuttal's Dictionary* a few years earlier, but not apparently before that. In contrast a *sprynge* of teal appears in Egerton's manuscript of 1452, whilst the terms *rush*, *trip*, *flight* and *company* have certainly been around since H.C. Folkard's *The Wildfowler* in 1859.

The moorhens illustrated are common birds of lakes, ponds, canals and rivers. Breeding birds are fiercely territorial and prefer their own company. At other times, particularly in hard weather, flocks of up to forty birds will group together.

Loomery
of guillemots

There are three species of guillemot which may be encountered around British shores. The scarcest of the three is an Arctic bird, Brunnich's guillemot. It is only an occasional winter visitor to this country but its Latin name, *Uria lomvia*, may well have given rise to the collective noun *loomery*. Another more plausible possibility is that it derives from the northern dialect term for the bird, 'loom'. The term applies strictly to a nesting colony of guillemots.

The common guillemot and the black guillemot make up the three species. They are members of the auk family and are birds of the sea and coast. Guillemots are very sociable birds and it would seem therefore most appropriate that they have a company term, and yet the guillemot is missing from many lists of collective nouns. Certainly the guillemot is not traditional sporting quarry and did not therefore appear in many of the earlier sporting books.

Loomery is only one of two terms recorded for guillemots. The other is *bazaar*, and could well relate to the hustle and bustle of the nesting colony of guillemots, which resembles the packed throngs of a busy market. Every available space is taken up on suitable cliff nesting sites, with noisy nesting birds competing for the best location and bringing up their young surrounded by others of their kind.

The guillemot has perhaps the biggest colour variation in its eggs of any British bird. Although consistently pyriform (pear-shaped), eggs have different base colours with further different coloured spots, lines, streaks and blotches.

Murmuration of starlings

The company term *murmuration* appeared as *murmuracyon* in the fifteenth-century Egerton manuscript. It is hardly surprising that this collective noun is long-established; such sociable birds have always been associated with our towns and cities.

An equally old and established term is a *chattering* of starlings. Both collective nouns are intended to convey something of the noise which these garrulous birds make when they assemble in huge numbers for their winter roosts. Starling populations, however, have not always been so healthy. At the beginning of the nineteenth century their numbers were in serious decline. They are now fully recovered.

Chattering also appeared in the Egerton manuscript as a company term for choughs, although this has been regarded as a misspelling of the more accepted term for choughs: *clattering*. A young starling is called a *stare* (also an Irish name for the adult birds), and this term is also one of the company terms used for owls.

The starling has beautiful plumage which changes with the seasons. Its beauty often goes unrecognised owing to our familiarity with the species. T.A. Coward called the starling an 'avian humorist', and indeed the bird has comical attributes. The male, perched perhaps on top of a chimney pot, may be heard not only to chuckle and chatter, but also on occasions to make the liquid call of the curlew. A great mimic, the starling can repeat a variety of different sounds, and not just those necessarily made by other birds. Even machines like garden mowers can be imitated!

Nye of pheasants

Pheasants are not indigenous British birds. They initially came from Asia, but were successfully introduced to many parts of Europe and North America. There are many different species of pheasant, and even those which are now regarded as wild in Britain take different forms. These latter birds originate from many different types which include the common pheasant (with no white collar) from Armenia, the Chinese ring-necked pheasant (with incomplete white collar) from Eastern China and Pallas's pheasant (which has a complete broad white collar) from Manchuria. All forms have freely interbred producing a wide variety of birds with collars in varying degrees of white.

Legend has it that the pheasant was introduced to Europe by Jason and the Argonauts. The exact time of its introduction to Britain is disputed. Until recent times, it was assumed that the Romans brought the bird here, but archaeological evidence seems now unable to prove this. Certainly there is documentary evidence of the pheasant being in Britain before the twelfth century. What is not disputed is the pheasant's reputation as a game bird, and it has always been reared as such. Its beautiful plumage is matched by its flavour and suitability for the table.

There are many variations in the spelling of the collective noun, including *nide*, *nie* and *ny*. The word means a hatch or nest of pheasants and relates specifically to the young. C.E. Hare maintains that 'a *nye*' should be 'an *eye*', arguing that *eye* is the Old English word signifying a brood. It has also been maintained that the word is derived from the French word *nid* meaning nest. Other company terms are *brood* for a family of pheasants, *bouquet* as a general gathering and *brace* for a pair of shot birds.

Parliament *of owls*

Owls have always held a special place in our hearts. Their faces, with their large forward-facing eyes, have almost human characteristics. Their nocturnal habits, silent flight and haunting calls have at the same time lent owls a certain mystery. Owls have been identified with wisdom and sagacity; the wise old owl in the gnarled oak is a popular image from children's literature.

There are about one hundred and thirty species of owl in the world. Six of them have nested regularly in the British Isles. The owls illustrated are tawny owls, also called brown or wood owls. It is *their* call, often wrongly quoted as *too-whit-too-whoo* (this representation combines both male and female calls) which has come to symbolise the call of all owls, even though the call of many bears no resemblance. Numerous ghost stories have their origins, for example, in the chilling shriek of a barn owl flying over some rural graveyard!

The term *parliament* is not included in many early lists as a collective noun for owls, and yet its definition as a group of owls appears in present-day dictionaries. This is in contrast to other terms which have no current dictionary reference, yet are well documented from the early books. *Parliament* appears more often as a company term for *rooks*. Groups of owls have also been referred to as a *stare* of owls (*stare* being in addition a term for a young starling).

Different species of owl group together in varying degrees. All of our resident owls except one are typically to be found as individuals or in pairs. The exception is the long-eared owl which can be found in communal roosts during winter to form a true *parliament* of owls.

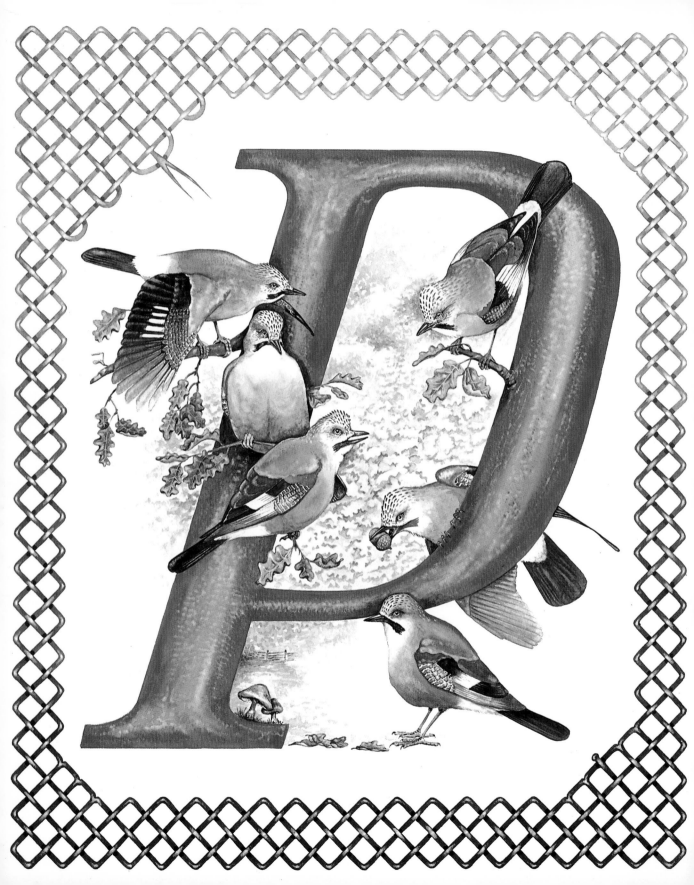

Party of jays

The jay is the most colourful member of the crow family. Often shot as vermin, it is loud and raucous, the hooligan of the woodland in which it lives. One is far more likely to hear the harsh screaming of the jay than to see the bird, despite its distinctive chestnut flanks, white rump and blue wing-flashes. Its retiring habit and love of the treetops means that only sharp-eyed observers will regularly see it.

Jays are especially fond of beech mast and acorns; indeed, they have been said to play a significant part in oak tree propagation through their habit of food-hoarding.

Jays are not as sociable as some other members of the crow family, for example their relative the rook. Jays tend to become territorial in the breeding season, when even non-breeding birds will not be tolerated. At other times, however, jays will often form groups which may be especially large if the acorn crop fails and food is scarce.

There are two recorded collective nouns. *Party* is the less well-known, the other being *band*. This latter term was perhaps first quoted in the American *Pacific Sportsman* magazine of 1929, and indeed now appears in most lists. A *party* of jays is certainly referred to in the 1967 book of collective nouns by B. Wildsmith, called simply *Birds*.

Raft of duck

There are many company terms for wildfowl in general and ducks in particular. *Raft* is not one that has references in the very earliest of sources, but is currently accepted as a term for ducks on water. Such ducks have also been referred to as a *paddling* or a *bunch* of ducks. When in flight ducks are referred to as a *team*. Terms which seem not to be specific about the ducks' position include a *trip*, *plump* and a *knob* or *little knob* of duck. Groups of pochard particularly are known as a *rush* or a *diving*.

The onomatopoeic term *dopping* is applied solely to sheldrakes, although seemingly could be applied to all shelducks. The term is said to derive from their habit of disappearing suddenly under water if disturbed, making a *dopping* noise. (A short bobbing curtsey was known as a dop in East Anglia, so this may also have been an influence.)

The number of different collective nouns springs not only from the fact that ducks have always been a popular and largely accessible sporting quarry. Nor is it just to do with the large number of duck species which frequent both salt and freshwater habitats around Britain. It may also be because, unlike many other quarry species, particularly game birds, ducks will often be referred to simply by the generic term *duck*. This can give rise to confusion, and is reflected in company terms which sometimes are used for ducks generally, and at other times for particular individual species.

The ducks illustrated are long-tailed ducks. These are sea ducks which have different summer and winter plumages and are to be found around the northern coasts of Britain outside the breeding season.

Sedge

of bitterns

Bitterns share their two collective nouns, many of their habits and much of their own limited habitat with herons. It is regrettable, therefore, that they do not also share their fortunes. For the bittern is now an extremely rare bird in Britain with less than twenty breeding pairs. This is due primarily to the drainage and destruction of their reedbed home, but egg collectors and hunters have also contributed to its downward trend; indeed it became extinct as a breeding species towards the end of the last century, re-establishing itself from migrant flocks to peak in the 1950s before its further decline.

Its coloration gives it perfect camouflage in its dense reedbed habitat; it can also elongate its neck and body at times of danger to further blend into its surroundings. These factors, together with its natural skulking manner, make the bittern one of the most elusive of birds. Paradoxically, the patient observer may on occasions be fortunate enough to witness quite spectacular displays of behaviour, especially during the breeding season, and at other times, when birds may climb precariously and noisily to the tops of reeds with apparent disregard for caution!

The background to collective nouns for bitterns is similar to that for herons, the term *sege* first being recorded in the fifteenth century and subsequently interpreted as *siege*. In 1688 Randle Holme's book *The Academy of Armory and Blazon* not only misspelt *shegh* of herons, but also *seigh* of bitters (sic). Many lists today give both *sedge* and *siege* as company terms for both herons and bitterns, but *sedge* would seem to be more suitable for the bittern, reflecting the more specific habitat of the latter.

Siege *of herons*

Herons are represented in Britain by the grey heron. These are long-legged, long-necked birds of the waterside, which rather incongruously nest together in large trees. At other times they stalk the margins of waterways for their prey of fish, frogs and small mammals. They appear in the very early lists of hunting books owing to the fact that they were once a popular quarry for falconers, *heron-hawking* being a favourite sport.

Herons have at times been given two collective nouns: *siege* and *sedge*. They share both with the bittern, a bird with whom they also share a variety of habits. The company term was originally recorded in a mid-fifteenth-century manuscript and subsequently in *The Book of St Albans* in 1486 as *sege*. This was interpreted in turn as *siege*. A misspelling appeared as a *shegh* of herons in the 1688 book *The Academy of Armory and Blazon* by Randle Holme. Then in 1859 in a book by H.C. Folkard entitled *The Wildfowler,* the term was recorded as *sedge*. While most contemporary lists adhere to the original interpretation, some do quote the latter and some both.

The term *siege* has been recognised as relating to the patient way in which a heron will wait for its prey, just as an army will patiently wait for the surrender of the enemy under siege. The company term should not be confused with the name for the *place* where herons breed, i.e. a *heronry*.

Although it is most usual to see a solitary heron, they can also be sociable outside the breeding season. They will often feed in close proximity to each other, especially on coastlines during winter.

Trip *of dotterel*

A dotterel is a dullard or a stupid person; the bird of the same name is so called because of its supposed foolishness in letting itself be easily caught, and indeed the second part of the bird's Latin name *Eudromias morinellus* means 'little fool'. The name given to it in Norfolk of stone runner, after its habit of alighting on rocky outcrops, seems a kinder term for this delightful wading bird.

A member of the plover family, the dotterel was once prized for its flesh, and seemingly did allow itself to be taken too easily, for it is now scarce. Dotterel have been described as being fearless at their nests and very tame and approachable when on passage.

Dotterel in Britain are summer visitors or passage migrants to their remote mountain-top breeding grounds. Birds do still breed in Scotland and parts of northern England, but they are mainly seen towards the end of April and the beginning of May in small parties or *trips*. Although their breeding plumage may appear distinctive (only males are illustrated), dotterel can be very difficult to see on the ground.

The word *trip* is an accepted collective noun and one which is also applied to goats. It is well established and was first recorded in Osbaliston's book *British Sportsmen* in 1785. Although the bird itself may be obscure to anyone not involved with ornithology, the term *trip* is surprisingly consistent in turning up in most lists of company terms. This may well be because the bird was at one time much more commonly known, owing to the fact that it was regularly eaten.

Unkindness of ravens

One of the most powerful birds of legend, the raven is steeped in mythology and antiquity. The word *raven* itself has changed little from the Anglo-Saxon *hrafn*. Odin, the great Norse God of War, Victories and Death was also the Raven God. His two pet ravens would fly far and wide before alighting upon his shoulder to whisper news to him. Ravens live to a considerable age and have been known to repeat words in captivity. The tame ravens are a feature of the Tower of London and it is said that if ever the ravens should disappear from the Tower, the monarchy will come to an end.

The explanation of the collective noun is no less strange. It was thought long ago that the breeding ravens gave no parental care to their chicks. People imagined that they expelled the young from the nest, leaving them to fend for themselves until they saw that they were the colour they ought to be. If they were indeed a glossy black they were cared for. It was said that such *unkindness* was repaid by the youngsters, however, for when the parents were old and their beaks worn, their offspring would offer no help. The group term was referred to in the Egerton manuscript of 1452.

In their mountainous, or coastal cliff home, ravens do in fact show a real *unkindness*. They will often not tolerate other birds near them, and although they scavenge they will also kill small birds (often in the nest) and mammals with their massive bill.

Ravens often occur in quite large flocks consisting of immature birds and adults which do not hold territories.

olery of birds

Unlike most other collective nouns in this book, the term *volery* applies to a number of birds generally rather than to one particular species. There are a number of company terms for birds which fall into this category. The most common term for an assemblage of birds is *flock*, but other alternatives include *congregation*, *aviary*, *multitude*, *host*, on the water a *raft*, and that collective which forms the title of this book but which is applied just to *small* birds, *dissimulation*. The word *brood* is often used for the nestlings, chicks or young hatched from a *clutch* or *set* of eggs. Birds which breed together in large groups are said to form a *colony*. A male and female bird together are referred to as a *pair* and two dead birds (usually game birds) are called a *brace*. The collective noun which comes closest to being a direct substitute for *volery*, however, is *flight*. Indeed, some artistic licence has been exercised in the illustration, for according to C.E. Hare a true *volery* of birds ought to be in flight. The term *volery* first appeared in the Special *Daily Mail* Edition of *Nuttal's Dictionary*.

Other terms referring to flying birds specifically include a *wedge* of swans, an *exaltation* of larks and a *skein* of geese, while the term *flight* can refer to birds generally but also in particular to doves, dunlin, goshawks, larks, pigeons, plovers, pochard, swallows, widgeon, or woodcock!

A little owl is illustrated in the centre of the picture and clockwise around it from the top left are: a male pied flycatcher, a male white wagtail, a male bullfinch and a pair of long-tailed tits.

Wisp *of snipe*

The common snipe is a resident British wading bird whose numbers are significantly increased by winter visitors. It is also called the full or whole snipe which distinguishes it from the smaller jack snipe. It is a heavily streaked and patterned bird which means it is well camouflaged amongst the vegetation of the flooded fields and marshes which it frequents.

If the snipe is disturbed it flies with a rapid, low zigzag flight, then often rises high into the air. This distinctive, dodging flight has no doubt saved many an individual from the table, as it is a prized sporting quarry. Another distinctive feature of the snipe in the air is its ability to 'drum' its outer tail feathers in its territorial diving flights.

The snipe is generally, though not strictly, gregarious and has two group terms. The fifteenth-century Egerton manuscript first makes reference to a *walke* of snipe, a term repeated in *The Book of St Albans* and subsequently appearing as *walk* in many modern lists. The term is thought to refer to the snipe's characteristic method of movement! Chambers' Dictionary lists the same term for a flock of wagtails.

In 1785 Osbaldiston's dictionary-style book *British Sportsmen* listed the group term for snipe as a *wisp* or *whisp*. This is thought to refer to the fine, light zigzag flight of the bird, and appears equally often in subsequent lists. Indeed, this term is one of relatively few which have regular contemporary usage. Dead birds have been referred to as a *couple* or a *leash* of snipe.

A List of Terms

Birds	*Volery – Congregation – Flock – Assemblage – Flight – Party – Multitude – Horde – Host – Raft – Aviary – Brood*
Bitterns	*Sedge – Siege*
Bustards	*Flock*
Capercaillies	*Tok*
Chickens	*Peep*
Choughs	*Chattering – Clattering*
Coots	*Fleet – Covert*
Cormorants	*Flight*
Cranes	*Herd – Sedge – Siege*
Crows	*Murder*
Curlew	*Herd*
Dotterel	*Trip*
Doves	*Flight – Dole – Dule – Pitying – True Love – Piteousness*
Ducks	*Raft – Bunch – Paddling – Badelynge – Team – Sore – Safe*
Dunlin	*Flight*
Eagles	*Convocation*
Fieldfares	*Flock*
Finches	*Charm – Chirm*
Fowls	*Scry*
Geese	*Gaggle – Skein – Team – Wedge – Lag – Flock*
Goldfinches	*Charm – Chirm – Trimming – Trembling*
Grouse	*Pack – Covey – Brood*
Guillemots	*Bazaar – Loomery*
Gulls	*Colony*
Hawks(let fly)	*Cast – Leash – Flight – Couple*
Hens	*Brood*
Heron	*Siege – Sedge*
Hummingbirds	*Charm*
Jays	*Party – Band*
Lapwing	*Deceit – Desert*
Larks	*Exaltation – Flight – Bevy*
Magpies	*Tiding*
Mallard	*Sute – Sord – Flush*
Nightingales	*Watch*

Owls	*Stare – Parliament*
Oxbirds	*Fling*
Partridges	*Covey*
Parrots	*Company – Flock*
Peacocks	*Pride – Muster – Ostentation*
Penguins	*Rookery – Colony*
Pheasants	*Kit – Nye – Nide – Brood – Bouquet – Brace*
Pigeon	*Flight – Flock*
Plovers	*Stand – Wing – Congregation – Flight – Leash*
Pochard	*Knob – Rush – Flight – Diving – Bunch*
Poultry	*Run*
Ptarmigan	*Covey*
Quail	*Bevy – Drift*
Ravens	*Unkindness*
Redwing	*Crowd*
Rooks	*Parliament – Building – Clamour*
Ruffs	*Hill*
Sheldrakes	*Dopping*
Small Birds	*Dissimulation*
Snipe	*Wisp – Walk – Couple – Leash*
Sparrows	*Host – Tribe*
Starlings	*Murmuration – Chattering*
Storks	*Mustering*
Swallows	*Flight*
Swans	*Game – Herd – Wedge – Bevy – Tank – Team*
Swifts	*Flock*
Teal	*Knob – Spring – Bunch – Coil*
Thrushes	*Mutation*
Turkeys	*Rafter*
Waterfowl	*Sute – Bunch – Knob – Plump*
Widgeon	*Knob – Company – Trip – Bunch – Flight*
Wildfowl	*Bunch – Trip – Knob – Plump – Sord – Sute*
Woodcock	*Fall – Flight*
Woodpeckers	*Descent*
Wrens	*Chime – Herd*

Bibliography

Hare, C.E., *The Language of Sport*, Country Life, 1939

Partridge, Eric, *Usage and Abusage* 1947, New and Revised Edition, Hamish Hamilton, 1965

Hardy, Eric, *The Bird Lover's Weekend Book*, Seely Service, circa 1950

Thompson, Landsborough A., (ed.), *A New Dictionary of Birds*, Nelson, 1964

Wildsmith, Brian, *Birds*, Oxford University Press, 1967

Lipton, James, *An Exaltation of Larks or The Venereal Game*, Angus and Robertson Ltd, 1970

MacIver, Angus, The New First Aid in English, Robert Gibson, circa 1970

The Oxford Reference Dictionary, Clarendon Press, 1986

The Complete Crossword Companion, Chancellor Press, 1988

The Chambers Dictionary, New Edition, Chambers Harrap Publishers Ltd, 1993

Rees, Nigel, *Dictionary of Phrase and Fable*, Cassell, 1994